What a Mess!

by Lucy McClymont

illustrations by Pauline Rodriguez Howard

Harcourt Brace & Company

Orlando Atlanta Austin Boston San Francisco Chicago Dallas New York Toronto London

"What a mess!" Mom said.
"All this for Camp Ladd?"

"Let's pack this mess," said
Dad. "Pass me the putt-putt
clubs."

Mom packed a chess set.
Matt wanted to add his mitt.

Jess wanted to add Mott,
Kitt, and Fudd.

"Where's Miss Bliss?" asked
Bess. "She was on the grass!"

"Don't fuss, Bess," Mom said.
"Do we have Miss Bliss?"

"Bess will be cross if we don't find Miss Bliss!" Jess said.

"That's odd," Dad said.
"Where's Miss Bliss?"

"Here's Miss Bliss," Bess said.
"She was on the grass."

"What a mess!" Jess said.

"Camp Ladd, here we come!"
said Mom, Dad, Matt, Jess,
Bess—and Miss Bliss.